MAKE A
FITNESS
PLAN

THE EXPERTS AT GOLD'S GYM

Enslow Publishing
101 W. 23rd Street
Suite 240
New York, NY 10011
USA

enslow.com

This edition published in 2019 by Enslow Publishing, LLC.
101 W. 23rd Street, Suite 240, New York, NY 10011

Cataloging-in-Publication Data

Names: The experts at Gold's Gym.
Title: Make a fitness plan / The experts at Gold's Gym.
Description: New York : Enslow Publishing, 2019.
| Series: Gold's Gym guide to fitness | Includes glossary and index.
Identifiers: ISBN 9781978506817 (pbk.) | ISBN 9781978506558 (library bound)
| ISBN 9781978506824 (6-pack)
Subjects: LCSH: Physical fitness—Juvenile literature. | Exercise—Juvenile literature.
Classification: LCC RA781.O949 2019 | DDC 613.7—dc23

Printed in the United States of America

To Our Readers: We have done our best to make sure all website addresses in this book were active and appropriate when we went to press. However, the author and the publisher have no control over and assume no liability for the material available on those websites or on any websites they may link to. Any comments or suggestions can be sent by e-mail to customerservice@enslow.com.

© 2020 Weldon Owen Publishing

Photo credits: All Gold's Glow Photography courtesy of Gold's Gym, with the following exceptions: First Design Global Inc. (p. 22 water bottle); ICON Health & Fitness (pp. 18, 19, 22 gloves); Pan World Brands Ltd. (p. 23 shaker cup); United Legwear & Apparel Co. (p. 23 flip-flops); Pinpoint Merchandising/Gold's Gear (p. 23 men's t-shirt, p. 31 shaker bottle); X-treme Activewear (p. 23 gym bag).

All other photos courtesy of Shutterstock.com: Kostiantyn Ablazov (p. 33 dandelion); Africa Studio (p. 20 top); Amarita (p. 33 sesame seeds); anitasstudio (p. 34 blueberries); AVAVA (p. 10 top); baibaz (p. 33 fortified cereal); Goran Bogicevic (p. 42); Binh Thanh Bui (p. 33 kale, p. 34 broccoli, salmon); Elena Elisseeva (p. 34 oats); Fotokvadrat (p. 11 bottom); Ilja Generalov (p. 27 bottom); Brent Hofacker (p. 33 cabbage); Anna Hoychuk (p. 32 salmon); JurateBuiviene (p. 36); Kzenon (p. 41); Lecic (p. 29); leonori (p. 33 orange); Lisovskaya Natalia (p. 40); Lizard (p. 35 tomatoes); Lopolo (p. 27 top); masa44 (p. 43); Monkey Business Images (p. 38); Mutita Narkmuang (p. 32 plain yogurt); Maks Narodenko (p. 35 avocado); Novikov Alex (p. 34 top); Photosiber (p. 32 sardines); Pinkyone (p. 33 almonds); Andrey_Popov (p. 10 bottom); rprongjai (p. 33 black beans); Elena Schweitzer (p. 28); Syda Productions (p. 20 bottom); Timolina (p. 39); urfin (p. 11 top); Lua Vandoorne (p. 31 top); Teri Virbickis (p. 32 cheese); Valentyn Volkov (p. 32 milk); wavebreakmedia (p. 30); wmatka_Wariatka (p. 37).

All anatomical illustrations by design36/Shutterstock.com.

All other illustrations courtesy of Shutterstock.com: pking4th icon in upper right corner headings.

CONTENTS

INTRODUCTION
A TRADITION OF STRENGTH

In 1965, fitness enthusiast Joe Gold took the knowledge and expertise he'd gained while working out at the world-famous Muscle Beach and opened his first gym in Venice, California.

This first Gold's Gym featured homemade equipment and a can-do spirit that made it an instant hit with local bodybuilders. In 1977, the gym gained international renown when it was featured in the movie *Pumping Iron,* starring Lou Ferrigno and a Gold's Gym regular by the name of Arnold Schwarzenegger.

Joe Gold's passion for fitness was the driving force behind that original location's success. Today, that same passion can be found in the staff, trainers, and members at over 700 clubs across America and around the world in countries including Japan, Australia, Venezuela, Russia, India, the Philippines, and beyond.

Gold's Gym remains the go-to gym for celebrities and professional athletes—and anyone looking to get into the best shape of their life. No matter what your fitness goals may be, you'll find the latest and best equipment, classes, and services to suit your needs, whether that means getting ready for a beach vacation or looking to make major life changes.

But more importantly, at Gold's Gym you'll find a welcoming and supportive community. For more than 50 years, Gold's Gym has been showing people that strength comes in many forms. Joe Gold realized that every body has a unique journey to achieving their health and fitness goals. Today, we're still dedicated to helping you set and attain those goals, in the gym and throughout your life.

It might happen after a period of indulgence—the winter holidays or a summer vacation trip—or just come gradually, after too much time on the couch and at the fridge. You look in the mirror, and you barely recognize the person you see.

Have you gained some weight? Lost muscle tone? Is your posture drooping, or do you just appear a bit weary, even depressed? These are the signs, sure indicators that it's time to hit the gym and to start monitoring your diet. But what if you're unsure of how to prepare properly for this upcoming fitness renovation? Your first step, of course, is to check with your doctor before beginning any exercise program.

CHOOSE THE RIGHT GYM

Choosing the right gym is paramount. You need a fitness venue like Gold's Gym that caters to all levels of clients—remember, today's beginner will soon become tomorrow's intermediate. Trainers should be knowledgeable and supportive, and there should be a choice of several, so you can find the personality that meshes best with your own. All equipment must be up to date and the level of cleanliness high. It helps if you determine what type of gym you seek—one that focuses on resistance training, one that gives you lots of cardio options, one with dance and yoga classes, or a mix of all three. Don't get drawn in by glossy advertising alone. Instead, pay each of your potential choices a guest visit, and talk to the members about the quality and depth of service. Nothing beats first-hand input.

FOCUS ON DIET AND NUTRITION

Once you choose a gym and start your new fitness regimen, it's time to focus on diet and nutrition—what to eat, when to eat, how to eat. Learn the value of different macronutrients like carbs, proteins, and, yes, even fats. Begin to understand the process of hydration and how to give your body the necessary amounts of H_2O it requires to properly function.

OUTFIT YOURSELF APPROPRIATELY

You will also need to outfit yourself in the right clothing and footwear—like tops and bottoms that wick moisture away and athletic shoes that have the right support—and stock a gym bag with toiletries, towels, water, and snacks. From there on, it's up to you to stick to your program, work toward your fitness goals, and maintain a positive attitude.

PICK YOUR HEALTH GOALS

Before starting any fitness regimen, you naturally need to determine your goals. Do you want to improve your looks, boost your sports performance, raise your endurance, or improve your overall health? Do you simply want to lose weight or also tone up and gain muscle mass?

Gold's Gym's GOLD'S PATH™ program breaks fitness goals into the four most popular categories so that you can more easily find your starting point.

 LOSE WEIGHT Get lean, lose inches, reduce body fat percentage, and keep it off.

 BOOST PERFORMANCE Increase endurance, gain functional strength,and improve sport performance.

 BUILD MUSCLE Gain strength, increase lean mass, or increase body definition.

 IMPROVE OVERALL HEALTH Get fit, reduce stress, move better, feel better, and live better.

Your workouts will vary based on each of these goals, so it's a good idea to consult a trainer at first to customize your regimen with these specific outcomes in mind. Once you start actively training, it helps to post an upcoming athletic event on your calendar—whether it's a 5K charity walk or a 50-mile bike-a-thon—to give you something concrete to work toward.

FIND THE RIGHT PLAN FOR YOU

The challenge to creating a fitness program is avoiding the latest here-and-gone fads and finding a plan that makes you feel great—and then sticking with it. The Gold's Gym Challenge is a 12-week full body transformation contest exclusively available to Gold's Gym Members. Not a member? Visit your local Gold's Gym where a personal trainer can customize a 12 week transformation plan to jumpstart your fitness journey.

Exercise is a proven way to get in shape, stay fit, and improve your outlook. And the best part? There is a range of fitness options and workout tools to choose from. You might want to experiment with free weights, cardio training, dance classes, Pilates, yoga, running, swimming, martial arts, and biking, until you find the right combination.

Once you have a plan, stay realistic about your progress. Heightened expectations can sabotage any fitness plan—if you want too much too fast, you're likely to be disappointed. If you want to obtain results faster, talk with a trainer. He or she can point out the level of improvement you should be seeing and ease any concerns. A trainer can also help you tweak or expand your current program. So don't lose sight of your goals, and remember that, as with many disciplines, the slow way is ultimately the fast way.

EVALUATE YOUR LIFESTYLE

While formulating your plan, imagine your day-to-day life, and consider how your new regimen can benefit it. If you are mostly sedentary and sit at a desk all day, an exercise program could compensate for all that inactivity. If you are more physical, exercise will help you keep up with the demands, especially as you grow older. And even if you participate in any sporting activities during the week or on the weekends, working out will help you achieve that high level of fitness your sport requires. A successful exercise plan will even allow you to spend a few hours crashed in front of the TV—without feeling guilty.

To avoid falling prey to these typical excuses for resisting a visit to the gym, try these motivational tricks.

I FEEL TOO TIRED AFTER WORK. Schedule a morning workout or a lunchtime session with a buddy.

MY DAY IS TOO BUSY. Pencil an hour workout into your planner as if it were an important meeting.

I FEEL SORE AFTER A WORKOUT. Simply vary the body part you concentrate on during your next session.

I HAD TO MISS MY END OF WEEK SESSION. No regrets … just reschedule it. Don't fall into the common trap of giving up after one disappointment.

FIND YOUR STARTING POINT

Every fitness program should start with establishing a baseline to evaluate future improvements. Start with the Gold's Gym fit test. The 10- to 15-minute test includes five exercises—crunches, push-ups, a pull-up for men or a bent-arm hang for women, squats, and a bench step test. Your results will generate a Fit Score, which you can use to track your health the way you use your body-fat index and cholesterol levels to help you track wellness issues. Your score indicates your level of fitness compared to Americans your age, and the test is free.

Ask the EXPERT
HOW DO I STICK TO A FITNESS PLAN?

Looking for ways to stick to your program? Here are some smart, stick-to-it strategies provided by the experts at the Gold's Gym Fitness Institute.

TELL FRIENDS Share your health and fitness goals with friends, family, or online; it helps to have a support group from the get-go.

TAKE A PIC Display an unflattering photo of yourself in plain sight to remind you of the cost of slipping.

TRASH THE BAD Purge your home of unhealthy, tempting foods. Make it easy on yourself, and stock up on healthy choices.

CAN THE EXCUSES Create a no-excuse mind-set—stash workout clothes in a bag or in your car's trunk.

TRICK YOURSELF Tell yourself you only need to do a half hour of work—then stay for an hour.

CHANGE UP YOUR MUSIC Experiment with a variety of music mixes to keep yourself engaged and upbeat while you work out. Switch it up when it becomes routine.

PUSH HARDER Push yourself to go the extra distance when you are tiring during a run or workout routine; just think how good you'll feel if you finish. Plus, you'll have momentum for the next time.

MAKE FRIENDS Make gym buddies who will expect to see you there for workouts or classes.

STEP ABOARD

Monitoring your progress is a regular part of any fitness program, so your weight losses or gains should be checked and recorded every week or so. The best way to do this is with a quality scale that is as accurate as possible. There are three basic types to choose from.

BALANCE SCALE This is the upright scale with adjustable weights that is found in your doctor's office or at the gym. Balance scales are quite accurate, but expensive.

DIGITAL SCALE Electronic digital scales with lit displays are accurate and easily portable. They operate on batteries or even on solar power. If the batteries are low, readings may be inaccurate. Some digital scales also offer additional features, like readouts with information about weight-related topics such as your percentage of body fat.

SPRING SCALE With these traditional scales, you step onto a platform, your weight compresses a spring, and a needle points to your weight. They are fairly reliable and can be recalibrated to zero with a knob or button; they cannot take much rough jostling, however.

MEASURE BODY FAT

These days, there are also several types of devices that measure the percentage of fat in your body. Although there is not a lot of research yet on just how this number relates to your general health, it may be an indicator of your chances of a weight-related ailment.

BODY FAT SCALES There are home body fat scales that use bioelectrical impedance (BIA) to gauge mass, water, and fat by sending an electrical current through your body and timing how long it takes. At present they are considered unreliable—drinking a lot of water can change readings by 10 percent.

HANDHELD BIA DEVICES These easy-to-use devices are often used in gyms, but they suffer the same reliability issues as body fat scales, and are often costly.

CALIPERS Caliper gauging, also known as the "pinch test," measures skin thickness at different places in your body. The resulting numbers are then plugged into a formula that estimates body-fat percentage based on age and gender. The pinch test is fairly accurate, but it can't be done properly without assistance, and it only measures subcutaneous fat.

HYDROSTATIC WEIGHING The most accurate readings of body fat come from hydrostatic weighing—which means you sit on a special stool underwater and expel as much air as possible while the machine weighs you. Check with a local university to find a facility that offers it. New high-tech machines that are nearly as accurate as hydrostatic weighing (that allow you to stay dry) are now offered at some gyms.

TAPE YOUR PROGRESS

Keeping track of your body measurements is essential. To start, go to your local Gold's Gym and get a full fitness assessment (all good gyms should provide this for free).

GET MEASURED Whether you are joining the 12-Week Challenge or just starting up a general fitness program, schedule a visit to a Gold's Gym to get your vitals down on paper. Be sure you bring along shorts (men) or a bathing suit (women) for your "before" photo. It will help inspire you to get in shape and keep the momentum going. A trainer will note the following:

- Weight
- Waist
- Thigh
- Hip
- % Body fat

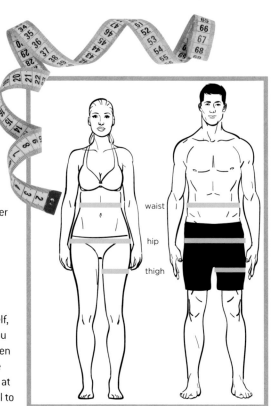

To make the most of this data, you can also measure yourself weekly at home. Rather than just weighing yourself, taking measurements is the most accurate way to tell if you are shaping up. You might see a loss of an inch or more, even if your weight isn't budging. That's an indication that you're making progress—losing fat and gaining muscle. Measure at the same time of day (and be sure to keep the tape parallel to the floor). Measuring also allows you to calculate your hip-to-waist ratio, which helps determine health risks. Record these numbers in your fitness journal from week to week.

SNAP SOME SELFIES

Scales and body-fat percentages may give you important numbers, but don't get stuck on those figures as your only measures of progress. It is actually your own figure that will give you a true sense of how far you've come on your fitness program. And the best way to judge this is to snap some photos of yourself before you even start your plan.

STRIP DOWN Strip down to just your skivvies or a swimsuit, and take or have someone take pictures of you from all four sides. Seeing yourself from all angles may be pretty disheartening, but don't try for flattering shots: in these "before" photos you want to see the real state of your body.

STICK 'EM UP Stick the photos in a spot you can't miss them, and then every few weeks, snap a new set to see just how far you've come. Eventually, there will come a day when you know for sure you are snapping a set of true "after" pics. These before and after photos are better than any scale for telling the story of your own transformation.

FIND THE RIGHT GYM FOR YOU

We may like to believe that we can become workout kings or queens at home, but sometimes it takes repeat visits to a dedicated space—a gym, health club, or athletic organization—for us to initially achieve real change. And the value of input or customized workouts from a professional trainer cannot be overstated. This is not to say a home gym won't offer you benefits, but many people find that first familiarizing themselves with all the equipment available at a commercial gym helps them determine how to best furnish a home gym.

There are certain steps you should take before purchasing a gym membership, including heeding these suggestions.

CREATE A MUST-HAVE LIST Draw up a list of must-haves—features or classes you would find in your ideal gym based on your established fitness goals. These could include a spacious free weight area, a variety of cardio machines, or a range of yoga classes. Even fitness newbies want to know their options.

RESEARCH ONLINE Avoid buying into hyped-up advertising or inflated fitness promises offered by competing facilities, and perform your own online research. Also, check online for feedback from satisfied or unhappy clients. Whatever gym you join should have an app so that you can link to the community and see class schedules, gym hours, and the like.

TAKE ADVANTAGE OF DEALS Look for introductory offers or coupon deals that allow you to try out gyms before signing up.

SCOUT THE LOCATION Location matters—Look for a gym near work if you plan on lunchtime workouts, or one near your home for early morning or evening sessions. A bonus would be if it's close enough to walk or bike to, for added cardio benefits.

CHECK OUT CLASS SIZES You don't want to feel packed into an overbooked class. Check out studio services, such as GOLD'SFIT® and GOLD'SCYCLE™.

MAKE SURE IT'S CLEAN Cleanliness should be an important factor, especially in the locker room and shower areas.

FEEL THE VIBE Ambience can affect attitude, so make sure the lights are not too bright, the décor too bold, or the music too loud. And always put substance above glitz or glamour. You'll do better in a supportive environment with a friendly community.

THINK *about it*
Some deals on gym memberships or personal training may be offered in January or September, but don't focus on joining a gym only then. Any time is a great time to get in better shape!

ASK THE RIGHT QUESTIONS

Suppose you've finally found what seems to be the gym of your dreams. But don't get the membership just yet. You might want to take a moment to look over the following checklist of questions and make sure everything is in order before you sign any of the paperwork.

HOURS Does your location offer a discount membership if you visit during off-peak hours?

EQUIPMENT What is the age of the equipment, and how often does it get replaced?

INSTRUCTION Are you shown how to use the equipment as part of the service, or is there a fee?

STAFF Is the staff certified? Are they trained to handle medical emergencies? Are there qualified personal trainers available?

AMENITIES What amenities or extras does the locker room provide, such as towels, shampoo, body wash, hair dryers, and Wi-Fi?

FEES Are all services included in your membership, or are there extra charges for certain classes or for the use of special equipment?

EXTRAS Do members get discounts on massage therapy or other extras?

CANCELATION What do you need to do in order to cancel? Are there penalty fees?

Like any sport or athletic pursuit, the fitness world has developed its own language. Your trainer may use words or phrases that are unfamiliar to you, or other members may use slang expressions you don't understand.

REP Repetitions; how many times you complete a single exercise in a row: "I did 12 reps of a bench press."

1RM (ONE-REP MAXIMUM) The maximum amount of weight you can lift in a single repetition.

SET A group of repetitions done without stopping.

SUPERSET A combination of complementary exercises done back-to-back in one "superset" with little to no rest.

FAILURE The point at which you cannot do one more rep. Reaching failure is believed to encourage muscle growth.

SPOT When someone assists another person with an exercise.

RESISTANCE TRAINING Any exercise using resistance, like weights, machines, medicine balls, or elastic bands.

SELECTORIZED MACHINES Also known as universal machines, refers to weight machines upon which poundage is selected by inserting a pin into the weight stack.

FREE WEIGHTS Typically refers to dumbbells and barbells.

BAR A long straight bar that holds plate weights.

EZ CURL BAR A curved weight bar often used for bicep curls.

COLLAR The attachment that secures the plate weights to a barbell or curl bar.

Not to worry. Just look over the following list of terms, and pretty soon you will be speaking fluent "gym" with all the other exercise buffs.

NEGATIVES Negative training is when the muscle lengthens during an exercise, called an eccentric contraction.

CIRCUIT A series of different exercises performed back to back with little or no rest.

PYRAMIDING Performing sets of downward or upward scaling reps or weight, such as 4 sets by 12-10-8-6 or 6-8-10-12

INTERVALS Training at a low intensity for a period of time, followed by a high-intensity period.

HIIT (HIGH-INTENSITY INTERVAL TRAINING) This interval strategy alternates periods of short, intense exercise with less intense recovery periods. Also known as Tabata™ training.

RECOVERY Refers to rest taken between exercises. Short recovery is best for fat burn and conditioning, long recovery is best for powerlifting and bulking.

DOMS (DELAYED-ONSET MUSCLE SORENESS) The pain and stiffness felt in muscles several hours to days after unaccustomed or strenuous exercise.

MAXIMUM HEART RATE Calculated by subtracting your age from 220. It is used when determining your training zone.

TARGET HEART RATE A good target heart rate for vigorous training is 70 to 85 percent of your maximum heart rate.

DISCOVER YOUR WORKOUT PROFILE

Before you commit to a fitness program and begin to create an exercise regimen that will truly work for you, it's helpful to understand what type of gym-goer you are. Just seven questions—crafted by Gold's Gym Fitness experts—can help you zero in on your workout profile.

Are you the grinder, who's allowed your workout to get a little stale? Or maybe you're a little too laid-back, showing up at the gym, but not really putting in the effort. You might be a real workout warrior, who makes fitness a priority; a fledgling who has a lot to learn; or the butterfly who uses the gym as just another social venue. Once you know your fitness personality, you can calculate how to get the most from your gym time and how to mix up your routine for a better workout.

HOW WOULD YOU DESCRIBE YOUR PERSONALITY IN GENERAL?

A. Dependable, organized, and steady

B. Agreeable, fun-loving, and pretty mellow

C. Intense (at times), motivated, and definitely adventurous

D. Shy with strangers, but warm and generous with friends and family

E. Outgoing, easy to be around, and loyal

WHY DID YOU JOIN A GYM?

A. I missed the routine of daily practice, having played a lot of team sports when I was young.

B. Just seemed like the thing a healthy adult should do.

C. I couldn't afford to build a home gym.

D. I wanted to start doing more than just long walks.

E. My friends joined.

OUTSIDE OF THE GYM, HOW DO YOU STAY ACTIVE?

A. I'm always up for a pickup game.

B. I don't really stay active—that's why I go to the gym.

C. I do triathlons, 10K races—you know, all that fun stuff.

D. Maybe I'll take an afternoon walk or go for an easy bike ride.

E. I love to do charity walks with groups, or fun runs with my family.

WHAT IS THE EXTENT OF YOUR GYM KNOW-HOW?

A. I can pretty much jump on any cardio or weight machine in the joint.

B. I know what I need to know.

C. I know the next big fitness trend before anyone else.

D. It's passable. I've mastered a few machines and the treadmill.

E. Pretty good. And if I need help, I just ask one of the trainers.

HOW FAR IN ADVANCE DO YOU PLAN YOUR WORKOUT?

A. No need to plan—I've got my routine down pat.

B. I don't. I just let my mood decide.

C. Weeks in advance. Doesn't everyone?

D. I wait to see what cardio and weight machines are available.

E. I usually check in with friends to find out what their workout plans are before I start to plan mine.

WHAT DO YOU DO BETWEEN SETS OR CARDIO SESSIONS?

A. Towel down, grab a drink of water, and then keep going.

B. Send a text or check my e-mail.

C. Check my heart rate, and then get right back to work.

D. Look for a free machine that I already know how to use.

E. Stop to chat with a gym buddy.

WHAT ARE YOUR LISTENING/VIEWING HABITS AT THE GYM?

A. I plug in my headphones, turn on the music, and get to work.

B. I take TV over music—if I control the remote.

C. I spend free time carefully crafting workout playlists.

D. Sometimes I read books, sometimes I watch television. It's a toss-up.

E. I don't like wearing headphones—I feel like I'm tuning out the people around me.

MOSTLY As – DAILY GRINDER

You grew up playing sports and started at the gym early, but now you've settled into a routine that lacks variety and is so dull that you might even quit. Try new things, like biking or running to the gym to add some scenery. You can also take classes— boot camp or mixed martial arts work many muscle groups and also deliver mucho cardio. Or join a training group that simulates a sports league … anything to break out of your routine rut and restore your love of fitness.

MOSTLY Bs – LAID-BACK LIFTER

You visit the gym because you know you should, but your heart isn't in it—plus you aren't pushing yourself toward any fitness goals. But going to the gym is half the battle, so try taking a group workout class that incorporates weights and weight-room exercises like squats and curls to get more out of your gym time. Hire a trainer for a session or two, and create a road map for your fitness future. The key is seeing the gym as an ongoing commitment to your body, not as a daily duty.

MOSTLY Cs – WORKOUT WARRIOR

Fitness rules your life. Being active and healthy is one of your priorities, and you enjoy it. You don't need much workout advice, but you should slow down at times to let your body rest and enjoy a little variety. You're a high achiever with a regimented workout, but adding variety makes you stronger and works more muscle groups. Try a yoga class to give your muscles a good stretch, a Zumba® class for a fun twist, or a mixed martial arts class to punch up your routine.

MOSTLY Ds – FITNESS FLEDGLING

You're a recent recruit (even after a few years at the gym) who's still working to get in shape, so you're wary of trying unfamiliar machines or new classes. Yet discovery is really enjoyable. The problem is you get in a rut because you do only what you know— you're stuck in a safety net. Ask for a free physical assessment (most gyms offer them) to gauge your fitness level. Then consult a trainer on how to use a given machine properly, or approach a teacher if you're nervous about a certain class.

MOSTLY Es – GYM BUTTERFLY

Being social is half the reason you hit the gym. Working out while catching up with friends keeps you going back. You just need to ensure that between conversations, you really are burning calories. If your routine isn't showing results, cut back on the chitchat, and try circuit training. Cross-train on the bike and then the elliptical—and minimize your rest period. Get your workout done faster; you'll then have more time to socialize. Also consider recruiting your friends for a boot camp or cycling class.

CHOOSE
A TRAINER

A trainer is one of the most vital and helpful tools in your fitness toolbox. A good one will motivate and stimulate you, ensuring that your physique continues to improve. Choosing the right one for you is essential and also sets you at ease while doing so. A good trainer will literally have your back and wants optimum results for you.

CHECK THEIR EXPERIENCE It's a good idea for you to interview different trainers to get a handle on their individual areas of expertise and what modalities they are most qualified to teach—especially if you should have certain limitations. Perhaps you suffer from tennis elbow or experience recurring lower-back pain. You will naturally be looking for a qualified trainer who is equipped to work effectively in such situations, one who will not in any way worsen your condition.

CHECK THEIR PRIORITIES The qualifications of trainers may vary, but bear in mind that your safety and personal goals should always remain their top priority.

CHECK THEIR STYLE It's important to get a sense that a trainer is not going to push you beyond your realistic capabilities, especially in the beginning. There's a fine line between challenging clients and intimidating them—the best trainers know how to walk it.

CHECK THEIR PERSONALITY Perhaps you have engaged a highly qualified trainer to work with based on his or her knowledge and experience, but you soon discover your personalities just aren't meshing. He may be too humorless; she may be too critical. Finding someone simpatico—who is truly on your wavelength—allows you to feel confident while achieving real results.

BUDDY UP!

Working with a trainer can help you achieve your goals, but sometimes, when motivation starts to lag, choosing to buddy up with a friend or partner can be very productive.

COOPERATION This is a cooperative partnership: one party counts on the other, and vice versa.

COMPETITION Friendly competition is a great motivator. If one of you is stronger than the other, don't make your competitions about who can lift the most weight or perform the most reps. See which one can first top a personal best.

ACCOUNTABILITY Knowing that someone is waiting at the gym for you at a certain time will encourage you to keep to your workout schedule.

POST YOUR SUCCESS!

One helpful way to stay motivated during the sometimes frustrating fitness process is to post your success or progression on social media or an Internet site — Facebook, Instagram, Twitter, or your own blog, for instance.

Set aside your vanity for a bit, and post several of those not-so-flattering "before" pictures you've taken. Then, after you have maintained that gym-going lifestyle over the course of several weeks or months, begin to post your "after" progress pictures. This sharing of your fitness evolution will be the means of both patting yourself on the back for a job well done and helping to motivate others to begin their own fitness programs.

WORK OUT AT HOME

Once you have familiarized yourself with the equipment at your gym and feel that you are staying on a regular schedule, it might be time to consider creating another workout center at home. This gives you some backup if you can't get to the gym, and lets you share workouts with a spouse, child, or friend. A home workout center can't often compete with the range and versatility of a commercial gym, it does offer one valuable benefit—convenience. For simple but effective home workouts, try using some of the following low-tech equipment, which take up little room.

FREE WEIGHTS Weight-training tools, which help to increase strength and bone density, are a must for your home gym. Handheld dumbbells and small hand weights have multiple uses, including isolation exercises. Also consider a set of barbells and a basic bench or a floor mat.

RESISTANCE BANDS These giant rubber bands come in various levels of resistance, and are lightweight and portable. There are flat bands or tubular varieties, which you can attach to handles for easier gripping.

JUMP ROPES Very little can beat these schoolyard favorites for offering low-tech but highly effective cardio workouts. Gold's Gym offers a variety, including the 3-IN-1 Jump Rope that offers adjustable weight, length, and speed.

MEDICINE BALL These weighted balls are great for high-speed, high-intensity resistance training.

STABILITY BALL This large inflatable ball can be used for a host of exercises, and can also be utilized like a bench for support. Gold's Gym offers the StayBall, which is weighted with sand for greater stability.

COVER YOUR BASES

To cover a lot of fitness bases, little beats the one-stop workout station called the home gym. This versatile machine allows you to focus on multiple areas such as chest (press and fly), shoulders (press and raises), arms (biceps and triceps), legs (extensions and curls), back (lat pull-down and rows), and abs (resisted crunches). Features to look for include adjustable seats and legwork components, variable bench positions, and effective levels of resistance—at least 150 pounds (68 kg) worth. You can try out the Olympic-width Gold's Gym Rack and Bench (shown below) with adjustable uprights and safety spotters; weight plate storage; a squat rack; independent utility bench; flat, incline, and decline bench positions; six foam leg developers with Olympic sleeve; a rolled preacher pad; removable curl yoke; and exercise chart.

When factoring price, ask yourself how much you intend you use the machine. Portability is another factor: does it fold up, or do its size and weight make it impossible to move out of the way? Certain models can equal the footprint of a love seat.

USE A STAND-IN

You'd be surprised at how many items already in your home can be substituted for gym equipment. Try using canned goods for hand weights, a full laundry detergent jug in place of a kettlebell, a chair back as a support during leg raises, an ottoman or picnic table seat for bench dips, or a filled duffel bag for lifts and curls. Or fashion a length of cotton clothesline into a jump rope. For some people, kitchen counters are the perfect height for doing triceps push-ups or impromptu barre work.

SELECT YOUR HOME MACHINE

TOOLS of the TRADE

The following exercise machines, which focus on different goals and supply varying levels of impact, are all popular choices for home workout centers. Look for models with electronic displays that show heart rate, calories burned, speed, and incline or resistance levels and that also allow you to program customized workouts. **Note:** Make sure to keep young children away from any equipment with moving parts, even if it is not in use.

ELLIPTICAL MACHINE

With its circular up-and-down motion—a cross between a treadmill and a stair-stepper—this machine offers cardio benefits and also helps strengthen legs, hips, and glutes because you are able to increase resistance—or work out in reverse! Because it is nearly impact free, this machine is good for those with joint problems or weight issues. Gold's Gym has numerous models of ellipticals, such as the Stride Trainer 550i.

TREADMILL

The treadmill, a time-honored weapon in the home gym arsenal, makes up more than half the fitness equipment market. The running/rapid walking motion specifically affects cardio-respiratory health. Look for models that feature a flexible surface, speed and grade adjustments, and an emergency stop device, such as the space-saving Gold's Gym Trainer 520 that comes with 16 preset workout apps.

STATIONARY BIKE

There are two types of workout bikes—the flywheel models and the air or bike models (such as the Gold's Gym Air Cycle). An upright flywheel bike (like the Gold's Gym Cycle Trainer 300 Ci) resembles a normal bicycle, while the recumbent (like the Gold's Gym Cycle Trainer 400 Ri shown here) has an upright seat that offers back support. The cardio benefits are similar for both positions. Some deluxe models offer a choice of moving scenery and allow you to participate in group classes—remotely.

KEEP THESE MACHINES IN MIND

There a range of other popular home exercise machines available. Here are a few more to consider.

ROWING MACHINES A low-impact rower exercises all major muscle groups at once, fairly close to a total-body workout. Sleek new models feature digital readouts and use piston/hydraulic, flywheel, wind, or magnetic resistance. These machines have a long footprint; if this is an issue, look for models that fold up for easy storage.

CROSS-COUNTRY SKI MACHINES This machine, which simulates the striding, sliding motion of a cross-country skier, exercises both arms and legs, but remains easy on the knees. Look for a wide foot-bed for stability.

STAIR STEPPERS This machine, which simulates climbing stairs, is considered low impact, but some people find the strenuous action hard on the knees. Some machines offer hand grips to also work the arms.

GEAR UP FOR PERFORMANCE

Gym-centric fashion has been with us since the 1980s, and we now see entire clothing lines dedicated to the "athleisure" movement, even some with celebrity branding. Yet, the basic uniform of the serious gym-goer has not changed much over the decades—a tank top or T-shirt, and shorts or leggings. Comfort and performance are the current watchwords. Hi-tech fabrics have even turned the T-shirt and shorts look into a perfect combination of functionality and old-school style.

Specialty shops and online vendors devoted to workout gear, as well as department and sporting goods stores, offer lots of workout clothing, with elite brands, budget options, and all the choices in between, along with various fitness trackers. Check your branch for a Gold's Gym Pro Shop with classic and modern Gold's Gym apparel. Also check out goldsgear.com.

KEEP IT WITH YOU

Extras like handy pockets further amp up the functionality of today's gear—do you really want to juggle your smartphone and keys while you're running on the treadmill? If you haven't stashed everything in a locker at Gold's Gym, look for clothing with hidden pockets—on the side, at the back, front, or in the waist—and you'll want them zippered to keep your things put.

HANDLE WITH CARE

Even your gym clothes regularly get a workout—when you exercise, you are not only sweating, you are also shedding dead skin cells and body oils, so you need to remove both odors and grime when cleaning them. Yet proper laundering can pose some problems. Most exercise clothing is made of delicate synthetic stretch fabrics that need special handling—for one thing, they are not tolerant of strong detergents or fabric softeners. Always read the care labels carefully, especially for high-end brands.

Here are some pointers for getting the most life out of your hard-working gym duds:

RINSE OUT SWEAT Rinse out sweaty clothes while still at the gym, and place them in a zip-lock bag.

PRESOAK GARMENTS Remove sour odors by presoaking soiled clothing in a basin of cold water with 1 cup (237 ml) of white vinegar for 15 minutes. You can also add a cup of white vinegar to the rinse cycle.

AVOID SOFTENERS Avoid using fabric softeners on synthetics; they leave behind a coating that can lock in odors and damage delicate elastic fibers.

HOLD THE BLEACH Never use chlorine bleach.

TURN EVERYTHING INSIDE OUT Before you throw your workout clothes into the wash cycle, turn them inside out to protect colors and expose the most soiled areas.

MEASURE SPARINGLY Use slightly less detergent than recommended, and wash your load in cold water. Or look for detergents that are made specifically for workout clothing.

KEEP IT COOL Air-dry clothing or machine dry at the lowest setting. High heat can cause synthetic and stretch fabrics to shrink and lose flexibility.

WICK IT AWAY

No one wants to feel like a sweaty mess during a workout. Technology comes to the rescue with sportswear fabrics that have the ability to wick moisture away from the body. Here are some possible stay-dry options:

POLYESTER This is a popular, breathable synthetic, but it does retain odors and has a high "stink factor."

COTTON Natural cotton doesn't retain odors, but it tends to hold moisture, so use it for low-sweat activities.

NYLON This fabric is lightweight, silky, mildew-resistant, and wicks moisture to the surface of the fabric.

BAMBOO Eco-friendly fabrics made from bamboo pulp are lightweight, naturally wicking, odor-repellent, and also protect your skin from ultraviolet rays.

POLYPROPYLENE This synthetic is water-resistant, making it ideal for wet weather activities. Its fibers force body moisture to the surface, where it can evaporate.

ELASTIC FIBER Fabric blended with elastic fibers, like Lycra or Spandex, lend them both super stretch and support. These stretch yarns are breathable, wick moisture, and dry quickly.

START OFF ON THE RIGHT FOOT

The modern athletic shoe is a marvel of engineering, with dozens of sporting applications. For your basic gym workout experience, look for a cross trainer that offers stability, style, shock absorption, traction, and a wicking footbed. And look for a proper fit—a workout shoe should feel comfortable right away. If you are involved in activities like kick-boxing or dance classes, discuss specialized footwear with your instructor. The following are some things to look for when buying workout shoes.

FLEXIBLE UPPER A flexible, lightweight upper will keep you agile and light on your feet.

STABLE BASE A stable base will support your foot, especially during lifting movements.

REINFORCED TOE A reinforced toe supports your foot during moves like push-ups.

NONSLIP SOLE A nonslip sole gives you safe support during kicks, lateral movements, and jumps.

Ask the EXPERT

SHOULD I GO FOR COMPRESSION?

A recent boon for dedicated gym-goers is the advent of compression clothing. These super tight-fitting elastic garments are usually found as tops and bottoms, with a choice of short or long sleeves or compression leggings versus pants. There are also plenty of accessory pieces for arms and forearms, legs, and the knee and elbow regions.

Compression clothing is worn during and after strenuous or explosive workouts and is reportedly effective at easing soreness and speeding up muscle recovery. It is believed that it reduces inflammation—and the build-up of fluid and pressure—and increases blood flow to the affected areas, which removes the pain-inducing enzyme creatine kinase. Compression also helps speed blood to your heart after it has oxygenated your muscles—thus allowing you to train harder and do so for longer.

THINK *about it*

If you're making regular trips to the gym, be sure your sneakers can handle the heavy demands you're placing on them. Most workout shoes need to be replaced after approximately 100 hours of use.

STOCK YOUR GYM BAG

Don't get caught in the locker room with an oversized duffel filled with excess workout gear. Just stock your tote with these must-have items. These smart essentials will help you maximize your time at the gym.

WATER BOTTLE

Purchasing a high-quality, reusable bottle makes sense both financially (no overpriced bottled water) and environmentally (no plastic waste). Plus, insulated bottles will keep water or sports drinks cold and heated beverages hot. Look for models like the Gold's Gym Hydration Bottle with an easy-open snap lid.

BATTERY-POWERED PHONE CHARGER

What's worse than climbing onto the elliptical only to realize your iPod is kaput? By tossing a portable charger into your bag, you'll always have extra juice available to keep your music playing so that you can pace yourself during a cardio workout. Many of these chargers also work for cell phones and handhelds.

CHAMOIS TOWEL

These lightweight towels have been used by swimmers and divers for more than 20 years. A chamois towel is made of a highly absorbent hi-tech PVA material designed to dry your body more quickly than traditional, bulky cotton towels. Small microfiber towels are also effective during and after a workout.

RESEALABLE PLASTIC BAG

If you regularly squeeze in a morning workout at the gym before heading to the office, you don't want your dirty, sweaty gym clothes smelling up your tote—and all the other accessories inside it. Keep odors at bay by placing the gym clothes and socks you've worn in large, resealable plastic bags. These are available at most supermarkets and discount stores.

WEIGHT-LIFTING GLOVES

While you're weight lifting (or working out with other hands-on equipment) you'd probably rather obsess about your form, not blisters and calluses. Look for machine-washable fingerless gloves that are made of soft, durable leather or vinyl. Check your local Gold's Gym Pro Shop for a variety of styles, like the stretch mesh Tacky Training Glove—it comes in multiple colors for both men and women.

SHAMPOO AND BODY WASH

These multitasking products, which often feature a scent that is perfect for both men and women, save you from packing two separate bottles in your gym bag. Or look for travel-size bottles that don't take up room in your gym bag, and place them in resealable bags.

RECOVERY DRINK

It's important to repair your muscles with loads of protein and anti-inflammatory nutrients within 30 minutes of exercising. Take advantage of your gym's health bar or pro shop offerings, or bring drinks from home. Try Vanilla Créme Muscle Milk (select Gold's Gym Pro Shops) or shake up your own in a Gold's Gym Fusion Mixer or Basic Shaker Cup.

CLEAN T-SHIRT

There's nothing better than knowing a clean, dry T-shirt is waiting for you after a tough workout and a shower. Consider packing a pair of leggings or clean sweatpants, too. After all, do you really want to put your sweaty workout clothes back on? Check out the many styles for both men and women at your local Gold's Gym Pro Shop.

WORKOUT JOURNAL

You know it's important to keep track of your fitness goals—and, better yet, your progress. With a journal devoted to both exercise and general diet information, you'll be able to record the decisions you make and your victories, as well as jot down questions for trainers. Try the Gold's Gym Workout Journal, or, if you carry a tablet to the gym, you can plot your activities electronically.

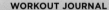

GYM BAG

You, of course, need a gym bag to carry all your gear. Check your local Gold's Gym Pro Shop for a wide selection of carriers, including classic duffel bags, backpacks, and tote bags.

RUBBER FLIP-FLOPS

You'll want to protect your feet on damp changing-room floors and when you hop into the shower or visit the sauna or steam room. Plus, it's nice to have something clean and dry to slip into after a hard workout. Make sure to keep your flip-flops clean with soap, water, and a spritz of disinfectant spray.

PACE
YOURSELF

Perhaps the hardest quality to cultivate during a long-term fitness plan is patience. In the results-based gym culture, you might push yourself to prove all that hard work is paying off, or you may want to demonstrate that you have the grit and determination to finish each exercise rotation quickly. This is especially true in a group environment, in which competition with others can override prudence. Yet, whether you are involved in high-intensity training or simply doing basic circuits, there are no gold stars for rushing to complete your reps. In fact, if you do rush, chances are you might finish only half of your intended goal. Not to mention, if you overdo it and get hurt, you won't be back on the machines for days.

WORK WITH
A TEMPO

To get the most from your workouts, use tempo to guide you. With an appropriate amount of weight for your strength level, you should be able to count two seconds on raising, then lowering, the weight. This lets you focus on the muscles being used and maintain good form throughout the set. If you have to take time off from the gym, gradually working back up in the amount of weight you use will also help you avoid overtraining or injury.

To build up your endurance and stamina in the gym, it's crucial to include cardiovascular exercise as part of your regimen. Cardio includes any movements or activities that increase your heart rate for an extended period of time. Long duration, sustained cardiovascular training, or intervals of cardio with short rests between should both be used to get the best results, and should be completed multiple times per week. Nutrition also plays a large role in your endurance during exercise, so pay close attention to nutritional recommendations (see items 031–033 for more details).

WARM
UP

Warming up is a frequently neglected (or even altogether forgotten) aspect of working out. Yet, it is important to have your muscles both warm and pliable for the often heavy workloads that will follow. A warm-up can be as simple as light dynamic stretching or a few minutes on a stationary bike in order to slightly elevate your heart rate and get those muscles and joints moving.

The tendency to dive right into an intense workout can result in injury due to the often excessive strain put on muscles and tendons at the sudden onset of explosive exercise. Taking a few minutes prior to your workout to properly warm up will not only help prevent injury, it will also properly prepare you for the work to follow. It's instinctive for a jungle predator to stretch out before pursuing its prey—and humans should learn from this behavior.

COOL DOWN

In the same way that warming up is vital to your gym longevity, cooling down is important as well … and for the same reasons. At the end of your workout, your muscles are pumped and filled with lactic acid—waste that has built up. Stretching at this time promotes the elongation of the muscle tissue, which helps transport vital nutrients more efficiently to your muscles, while aiding in the removal of the waste. Stretching will also help to keep you progressing and injury free.

Your greatest insurance in the gym is the care you give to your body by listening to it and offering it what it needs. Warming up and cooling down, though they may not seem glamorous, will keep you in this game for the long haul, and a few minutes before and after each session is a small price to pay for a lifetime of successful workouts.

GET AN INTRODUCTION TO PROPER NUTRITION

Nutritional science studies and interprets the interactions of nutrients, and other substances in food, in relation to their effect on the maintenance, growth, reproduction, health, and disease of an organism. Nutrition is a key element in fitness, health, and in exercise—you can't out-train a bad diet.

Food is made up of macronutrients—carbohydrates, fats, proteins, and water—that are required in large quantities, along with micronutrients—minerals, vitamins, antioxidants, phytochemicals, and intestinal flora—that are needed in smaller quantities. A balanced human diet is composed of these different nutrients in the right proportions. The wrong ratios—or critical omissions—can affect both physical and mental health.

Exercise may be a big part of fitness, but up to 75 percent of your gains in the gym are also going to be based in your intake of macronutrients and micronutrients. If you need solid advice, a nutritionist can help—and many gyms out there, including Gold's Gym, have trained nutritionists on staff to assist you.

MAKE SOME SIMPLE CHANGES

It only takes three simple ideas to change the way you think about eating—planning, fueling, and recharging.

PLAN AHEAD When you are involved in a weekly fitness program, you not only want to keep hunger at bay, you also need to keep energy levels steady. Nutritionists recommend three meals, plus two snacks, in the course of a day. Balancing the right proportions of dietary macronutrients will allow you to maintain both your weight and energy levels. Try to create menus that are heavy on the vegetables, fruits, and healthy, whole-grain carbohydrates, with considered amounts of lean protein and polyunsaturated or monounsaturated fats. Also be sure to drink plenty of water, because a healthy diet combined with proper hydration will positively affect your workouts—and your daily life.

FUEL UP Always eat before you exercise. This helps to prevent low blood-sugar levels and hunger pangs during a workout, as well as provide energy to your muscles. Three or four hours before your workout, prepare a small meal of complex carbs—a whole-wheat waffle with yogurt and blueberries, whole-grain cereal with low-fat milk and banana slices, or a parfait of kiwi and orange slices over low-fat vanilla yogurt topped with low-fat granola. You can also have a light snack one to two hours before your workout.

RECHARGE Any intense workout that lasts longer than an hour will deplete your body of carbs and fluids. A small meal eaten soon after will remedy this, as well as help aid in muscle repair and recovery—muscles are most receptive to replacing glycogen within the first two hours after hard exercise. indulge in a protein drink at the gym bar, and follow that with a full, balanced meal two hours later. Try a baked sweet potato topped with chili, white-meat turkey in a whole-wheat wrap, pasta with chicken and veggies, or eggs scrambled with peppers, onions, and spinach.

RETHINK YOUR EATING HABITS

Your workout plan should focus on two factors—eating smart and getting fit, in that order. Before achieving a better external physique through exercise, you need to start building up your body from the inside. This requires an awareness of the types of foods you should eat, those you need to avoid, and the supplements you may require.

Smart nutrition also means rethinking the ways you eat, the times and places you eat, and your attitude toward food in general. As your fitness regimen advances, you will likely find that many of your cravings have altered. You'll be less likely to indulge in salty or fatty snacks and become more concerned about the nutritional value of meals rather than simply the levels of satisfaction. Food will eventually become the ally rather than opposition.

MAKE SENSE OF MACRONUTRIENTS

Most nutritional guidelines indicate an approximate percentage of macronutrients—carbohydrates, proteins, and fat—humans require for optimal health, but their ratios are widely debated. Following a workout plan also affects these numbers.

In general, to maintain a healthy weight, women need 1,600 to 2,400 calories per day, and men need 2,000 to 3,000 calories. Age, sex, and level of activity, along with diet and fitness goals are among the factors that determine how those calories are portioned among the macronutrients. A nutritionist can answer a variety of questions for you on suggested intake amounts based on your goals, whether you're working toward weight loss, body building, or general fitness. Whatever breakdown of nutrients you follow, focus on variety, nutrient density, and healthy amounts of all food groups. Limit calories from sugars and saturated fats, and reduce sodium intake.

This chart below gives you sample recommended ranges of percentages of daily calories for varying goals, whether you want to build muscle, lose fat, or maintain the shape you're in.

NUTRIENT	MUSCLE BUILDING	FAT LOSS	MAINTENANCE
CARBOHYDRATES (4 calories per gram)	40 to 60 percent	10 to 30 percent	45 to 65 percent
PROTEIN (4 calories per gram)	25 to 35 percent	40 to 50 percent	10 to 35 percent
FAT (9 calories per gram)	15 to 25 percent	30 to 40 percent	10 to 35 percent

CHOOSE YOUR CARBS

Carbs are one of the main nutrients in our diets, and the most important one for those who are following a workout regimen—they are not only the top food source for energy, but they are also a source of recuperation. The digestive system turns carbs—most commonly sugars, starches, and fiber—into glucose (blood sugar), which the body then converts to energy that supports bodily functions and physical activity. When choosing carbs, remember, the more complex the better.

SIMPLE CARBS Simple carbs, such as white bread, white rice, or refined sugars, interfere with fat metabolism, may contribute to fat gain, decrease the body's energy needed for prolonged activity, increase hypertension (leading to high blood pressure) and can create an energy roller coaster as blood glucose levels fluctuate.

COMPLEX CARBS These carbs, found in natural, high-fiber foods like whole grains, fruits, vegetables, and beans, are far better for you than refined foods because they get absorbed more slowly into the system, avoiding spikes in blood sugar and offering sustained energy. They also make you feel more satiated after a meal and less likely to snack.

PICK YOUR PROTEINS

Proteins are organic molecules made up of amino acids—the building blocks of life— that produce the enzymes, hormones, neurotransmitters, and antibodies that enable the human body to function. Proteins also aid in growth of muscle tissue. As food is digested, proteins break down in the bloodstream into individual amino acids that trade with other amino acids already located in our cells. This provides a supply of frequently replenished amino acids that are ready when needed. Some fitness buffs believe that if you beef up on protein—which contains 4 calories per gram—you will gain muscle. Although it's true that proteins rebuild and repair muscles, your body can only handle a certain amount; the rest turns to waste. So limit your intake to six to seven ounces of protein daily—even if you are an athlete.

COMPLETE PROTEINS These generally come from animal sources and include beef, poultry, fish, milk, eggs, cheese, and yogurt. Plant-based soy is also a complete protein.

INCOMPLETE PROTEINS This group is made up of vegetable sources that don't contain all nine essential amino acids, or don't have sufficient quantities of them. They include nuts, seeds, beans, and grains. They should, ideally, be combined with each other to complete the essential amino acid profile—for example, you can pair rice with beans, toss some almond slivers over a leafy spinach salad, or spread peanut butter on whole-grain toast.

OPT FOR VEGAN PROTEIN

If you're a vegetarian or vegan, there's no need to become protein-deprived. There are plenty of plant-based foods that supply the necessary protein needed for a healthy diet.

LOWER-CALORIE SOURCES Foods made from soybeans offer some of the highest amounts of protein: tempeh and tofu contain 15 and 20 grams per half cup, respectively. Actual soybeans, known as edamame, are also a rich source. Legumes, like peas, beans, and lentils, make an excellent meat substitute. Peas contain 7.9 grams of protein per 8 ounces, about the same as a cup of milk. Although grains contain a relatively small amount of protein, quinoa (which is actually a seed) offers more than 8 grams per cup, as well as all nine essential amino acids. Not surprisingly, this little seed is often called the "perfect protein."

HIGHER-CALORIE SOURCES Nuts, which provide healthy fats and proteins, are invaluable in a plant-based diet. They can be high in calories—roasted almonds, cashews, and pistachios contain 160 calories per ounce along with their 5 to 6 grams of protein—so choose varieties that are raw or dry roasted. Nuts and seeds make an ideal protein-based snack for those times at work when you skipped lunch or when you're heading to the gym and need a nosh. Sesame, sunflower, poppy, chia, hemp, and flax are especially good choices because they also contain fiber, minerals, vitamin E, and omega-3 fatty acids. With all those calories, however, stick to recommended portions.

Tracking your nutrition can be time-consuming, but some people love to calculate all of their macros. Even if you're not the type to do so, the good news is that there are great apps that can make tracking almost effortless. Some will help you make sense of nutrition labels, which can steer you to better choices at the grocery store; others can help you track your calorie intake. Some even will send you reminders and motivational messages.

- Calorie Counter Pro
- Carb Master Free Daily Burn
- DietHero
- Diet Point Weight Loss
- Diet Watchers Diary
- FatSecret
- Fooducate
- My Diet Coach
- MyFitnessPal
- Nutrino
- PRO MyNetDiary
- Shopwell
- SparkPeople Calorie Counter and Diet Tracker
- Thryve

DON'T FEAR THE FAT

Fat often gets a bad rap as the culprit behind unwanted weight gain. However, a balanced diet requires this macronutrient: fat supports some body functions and helps to dissolve certain vitamins. As with carbs, there are different types—and it is important to know which of fats are beneficial and which are the ones to avoid.

THE BAD Saturated fat comes from animal sources, like red meat, poultry, and dairy products, and has been linked to higher levels of cholesterol and high-density lipoprotein (LDL), which can increase the risk of cardiovascular disease. Trans fats occur naturally in many foods, but most are made from oils using a process called partial hydrogenation. Trans fats also increase LDL levels and lower beneficial high-density lipoprotein (HDL). They are typically solid or semi-solid at room temperature.

THE GOOD There are healthier fat options, including monounsaturated fat (MUFA), which improves cholesterol levels, and polyunsaturated fat (PUFA), found mostly in plants or oils. Healthy fats, like olive, safflower, peanut, and corn oil, remain a liquid at room temperature.

THE VERY GOOD Heart-healthy omega-3 fatty acid is a PUFA that can actually decrease the risk of coronary artery disease. Sources include oily fish like salmon, tuna, sardines, and herring, as well as avocados, flaxseed, canola (rapeseed) oil, nuts, and many spices.

SUPPLEMENT SAFELY

Sports supplementation has become "big business"—and for good reason. Supplements do work in many cases. Products like protein powders, fish oil, or branched chain amino acids can fill in small deficiencies and increase performance, depending on the individual. Weight loss supplements or performance enhancers, on the other hand, contain powerful drugs that can be risky to ingest. And detoxes (diuretics) and laxatives offer only short-term results. In most cases, a healthy diet provides all the nutrients you require; sports supplements are meant to augment this balanced diet, not replace it.

When it comes to the micronutrients, although there are a mind-numbing number of vitamins available on the shelves of your pharmacy or health food store, most people find that taking a high-quality multi-vitamin serves them just fine. Unless you are diagnosed with a specific deficiency, your over-the-counter multi offers you the optimum amounts of your daily requirements in a single convenient tablet or capsule. Look for special customized products for men, women, and seniors.

POWER UP WITH PROTEIN POWDER

Commercial protein powders allow you to prepare health shakes whether you need a satisfying snack or a meal replacement. These powders are typically made from high-quality sources like egg albumin, milk (whey and casein), and soy, plus they tend to contain all the essential amino acids that our bodies can't make, but which need to be part of our diets.

EGG ALBUMIN These protein powders, made from egg whites, are a high-quality source of protein. These kinds of powders were the original standard for body builders.

MILK PROTEINS Casein and whey protein powders are made from cow's milk—casein from the curds and whey from the liquid portion. The powders tend to have a slow rate of digestion.

SOY These powders offer a nutritious plant-based source of complete protein.

UP YOUR INTAKE

Although our diets should ideally supply our daily protein requirements, there are times when gym-goers might need the extra protein offered by these powders.

WHEN STILL GROWING Teens tend to need more protein as they work out or take part in sports.

WHEN BEGINNING AN EXERCISE PROGRAM
If you're just starting to build muscle, your body will need extra protein.

WHEN INCREASING WORKOUT INTENSITY
If you're amping up at the gym or prepping for a race, consider increasing protein intake.

WHEN RECOVERING FROM INJURY Consuming more protein can help you heal more quickly.

Signs of low protein intake include weakness during weight workouts, fatigue, and injuries that are slow to heal. Just bear in mind that 10 to 14 additional grams of protein a day will usually do the trick, yet some powders contain 80 grams per serving. That's simply too much, and breaking it down can be hard on the liver and kidneys.

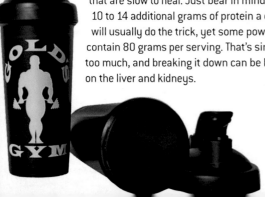

SHAKE IT UP

There are endless ways to make refreshing, healthy drinks from a basic protein shake recipe: two cups of liquid, fresh or frozen fruit and vegetables, nuts or seeds, and your choice of protein powder. The liquid can be water, milk—soy, almond, rice, or low-fat dairy—or yogurt. Seasonal fruits (such as pumpkins or peaches) or exotic types (like papaya, kiwi, or mango) are good additions. If you're wary of adding spinach or kale to shakes, you can include a flavorful fruit. The taste of berries is particularly effective for masking the greens.

If you're among the super health conscious, add flaxseed or oats for fiber and micronutrients, banana for electrolytes, low-fat Greek yogurt for probiotics, chopped or slivered nuts for fiber and unsaturated fats, and cinnamon or cardamom for high levels of antioxidants. Simply combine your chosen ingredients with a handful of ice in a bullet processor or juicer for a perfect frothy mixture. Or you can use a countertop blender to combine fresh fruit or purées with cold water or a creamy option like soy or almond milk. Just avoid anything too hard or granular.

Even if you don't have time to make your own, Gold's Gym has a smoothie bar to help you power up before your workout, or get extra nutrition after!

SMOOTHIE RECIPE APPS

If you need some inspiration to help you devise delicious pre- and post-workout smoothies, great recipes for super-healthy shakes will be at your fingertips when you search the following apps. Many give recipe-specific nutritional info and also allow you to share your favorite ones with family and friends.

Also check online on the Gold's Gym Strength Exchange for delicious and healthful recipes.

- *Green Smoothies*
- *Instasmooth*
- *Pocket Smoothie Recipes*
- *Primal Smoothies*
- *Protein Pow*
- *Protein Shake Recipes*
- *Superfood HD*
- *Whole Living Smoothies*

BUILD BONE

No matter your age, working out places a lot of demands on your body. To help compensate for this, muscles require a solid, supportive framework—which means a healthy, functional, and strong skeletal system.

Exercise can help you maintain your bones—weight-bearing physical activity can cause new bone tissue to form and allow you to achieve greater peak bone mass. It also allows you to improve muscle strength, coordination, and balance, which in turn helps prevent falls and related fractures. But first you shoudler make sure you are doing the utmost nutritionally to sustain your skeleton. The two chief nutrients required for this are calcium, which builds strong teeth and bones, and vitamin D, which improves calcium absorption and bone growth. They can both be found in these following food sources, among others.

MILK

Dairy products are high in calcium, and the calcium they contain is extremely well absorbed. So have a glass of milk—just 1 cup (237 ml) of moo juice supplies 30 percent of the daily requirement.

HOW MUCH CALCIUM?
306 mg in 8 ounces (237 ml)

CHEESE

No need to binge on it or slather melted cheese over everything you eat—just one portion of cheddar cheese the size of a pair of dice, for example, supplies 30 percent of your daily calcium needs.

HOW MUCH CALCIUM?
195 to 205 mg in 1 ounce (28 g)

PLAIN YOGURT

With only about 160 calories, 1 cup (237 ml) of this creamy favorite can supply 42 percent of the recommended daily amount of calcium and 20 percent of vitamin D daily.

HOW MUCH CALCIUM?
415 mg in 8 ounces (237 ml)

SARDINES

These small, canned fish, when packed with the bones, have surprisingly high levels of both vitamin D and calcium. They are also high in B12, B3, and B2. Serve in a pasta sauce or in salads.

HOW MUCH CALCIUM?
5 mg in 3 ounces (85 g)

SALMON

This delicious pink fish not only contains heart-healthy omega-3 fatty acids, a mere 3 ounces (85 g) of sockeye also supplies more than 100 percent of your daily vitamin D.

HOW MUCH CALCIUM?
20 mg in 5.5 ounces (154 g)

FORTIFIED CEREAL

Many of us love to start our day with a bowl of cereal. So, read the front of the box or the ingredient list to discover which healthy, whole-grain cereals offer you 25 percent of your daily vitamin D.

HOW MUCH CALCIUM?
100 to 1,000 mg in 8 ounces (226 g)

CABBAGES

Look to members of the cabbage family, like broccoli, kale, bok choy, cabbage, mustard, and turnip greens, for leafy sources of calcium. They also help build strong bones with folate and vitamin K.

HOW MUCH CALCIUM?
60 to 300 mg in 8 ounces (226 g)

DANDELION

Look no further that your front lawn for a fresh source of calcium. Dandelion is high in this mineral—ounce for ounce more than milk—and it's packed with other nutrients. Use the greens in salad.

HOW MUCH CALCIUM?
52 mg in 1 ounce (28 g)

ORANGES

Whole oranges are potent sources of calcium, and their ascorbic acid may also aid in calcium absorption. If your prefer this morning staple in a glass, look for varieties with added vitamin D or calcium.

HOW MUCH CALCIUM?
60 mg in 1 average orange

ALMONDS

These tasty nuts have a lot to offer. A ½ cup (118 ml) supplies you with 18 percent of the calcium you need each day. And they will also promote weight loss, colon health, and heart health.

HOW MUCH CALCIUM?
183 mg in 4 ounces (114 g)

SESAME SEEDS

If you want to get the calcium you need without eating animal products, try out these tiny seeds. Sesame also supplies other nutrients and minerals—including copper, manganese, and iron—and fiber.

HOW MUCH CALCIUM?
88 mg in 1 tablespoon (14 g)

EAT RIGHT ON A BUDGET

We are all familiar with supermarket sticker shock: a few basic food items like eggs, milk, bread, lettuce, and cheese leaves your wallet distinctly lighter. Food costs will keep escalating, so it's important to shop wisely.

USE APPS Check out the many smartphone and tablet apps—some are even free—that let you plan menus, watch your calorie intake, and find alternative food options.

CLIP COUPONS Sign up online for one of several services that offer you customized coupons for the healthy foods you prefer—low-calorie frozen meals, gluten-free products, or organic foods, for instance.

GO ORGANIC Many organic farmers or ranchers don't bother with the expense and red tape required to earn "certified organic" labels. So simply make sure the product packaging says organically grown, and you will pay about 50 percent less than for certified foods.

MAKE SOUP There are many ways to augment low-sodium soup and turn it into a nutritious meal: add seasoning, spices, vegetables, meat, pasta, or even scrambled eggs. Studies show that dieters are less likely to overindulge when starting a meal with low-fat soup.

BUY FROZEN VEGGIES Slash the high price of fresh vegetables (and fruits) by opting to buy frozen in bulk. Flash-frozen produce works well in soups, casseroles, quiches, pasta, and health shakes.

AVOID WASTE Think before you discard any leftovers. Bones or meat scraps can be used in making soup stock. Vegetables can be added to an omelette or processed with your morning smoothie. Consider buying storage bags or disks that slow spoilage.

DISCOVER SUPERFOODS

They may not actually be miracle cures, but so-called superfoods are nutrient-rich powerhouses that offer large doses of antioxidants, polyphenols, vitamins, and minerals. They may reduce the risk of chronic diseases and prolong life. People who consume superfoods tend to be healthier and thinner than those who don't. Superfoods are also easy to fit into your diet if they aren't there already.

BLUEBERRIES

These berries are full of phytonutrients that neutralize free radicals (agents that cause aging and cell damage). Their antioxidants may also protect against cancer and reduce effects of age-related conditions, such as Alzheimer's disease. Try sprinkling blueberries in your yogurt or granola, or add them to your morning health drink.

KALE

Phytonutrients found in kale appear to lessen the occurrence of a wide variety of cancers, including breast and ovarian. Scientists believe they trigger the liver to produce enzymes that neutralize potentially cancer-causing substances. Kale can be sautéed with olive oil and garlic or added to a vegetable smoothie.

BROCCOLI

Cruciferous vegetables like broccoli contain phytonutrients that may suppress the growth of tumors and reduce cancer risk. One cup (226 g) will supply you with your daily dose of immunity-boosting vitamin C and a large percentage of folic acid. Broccoli is a stir-fry star, but also try it as a salad ingredient.

OATS

Oats are a rich source of magnesium, potassium, and phytonutrients. They contain a special type of fiber that helps lower cholesterol and prevent heart disease. Magnesium works to regulate blood-sugar levels, and research suggests that eating whole-grain oats may reduce the risk of type 2 diabetes. Oats can be used as a breakfast cereal, in baking, or mixed into meatloaf.

BLACK BEANS

A cup (226 g) of black beans packs 15 grams of protein, with none of the artery-clogging saturated fat found in meat. Plus, they're full of heart-healthy fiber, antioxidants, and energy-boosting iron. They make an excellent low-calorie soup or a piquant veggie dip.

SALMON

Salmon contains omega-3 fatty acids, that the human body cannot produce by itself. Omega-3s reduce inflammation, improve circulation, increase the ratio of good to bad cholesterol, and may even slash cancer risk. Salmon is also a rich source of selenium, which helps prevent cell damage, and several B vitamins. Try an apple-and-horseradish glaze on baked salmon.

AVOCADO

With its bad rep as too fattening, the avocado is so often overlooked. Yet along with its deliciously creamy taste, this superfood is filled with healthy fats and essential nutrients: oleic acid, lutein, folate, vitamin E, and glutathione to name just a few, that can help protect your body against heart disease, cancer, and eye and brain diseases. Toss a few chunks into a smoothie or eat it as a side with egg dishes in place of potatoes.

TOMATOES

These popular fruits contain lycopene, an antioxidant rarely found in other foods. Studies suggest that it could protect the skin against harmful UV rays, prevent certain cancers, and lower cholesterol. Plus, tomatoes contain plenty of potassium, fiber, and vitamin C. Try them in a tasty avocado, lettuce, and tomato sandwich, which contains another superfood—avocado!

SHOP SMART

The best way to avoid unhealthy foods, like sugary cereals or salty snacks, is simply not to buy them. You can't be lured to cheat by something that is not inside your cupboard. Always shop with a prepared list, and stick to it for the most part. Naturally, if something healthy, natural, or organic is on super-sale, it makes sense to add it to the cart. Perhaps most important of all, never shop for food while you are hungry; too many tasty treats will tempt you to depart from your list. Always schedule grocery excursions after breakfast, lunch, or dinner, when you are feeling satiated.

AVOID GROCERY GOOFS

Many food items that shoppers believe are healthy choices have high—or hidden—calories as well as excess amounts of sugar, salt, or preservatives.

ENERGY BARS Don't let the advertising fool you—these are not legitimate alternatives to a healthy snack. Even if they do contain vitamins, minerals, and fiber, they are sweet treats, not health food. At least opt for varieties that offer whole grains, nuts, or dried fruit, and not those with chocolate or caramel.

GRANOLA Manufacturers insist this dense, whole-grain cereal is a healthy breakfast alternative, but they often add honey, sugar, and oil. A quarter-cup serving can have 150 calories—before you even add milk. Instead, try using granola as a topping lightly sprinkled on yogurt, health muffins, or oatmeal. And if the package lists three or more types of sugars in the ingredients (honey, brown sugar, and molasses, for instance), give it a pass; health food stores usually stock less-sugary alternatives.

TRAIL MIX Also known as GORP ("good old raisins and peanuts"), this snack is popular with both kids and adults. Yet, it was originally meant for hikers undertaking rigorous activity, not TV-tray noshers. The calorie-dense nuts and dried fruits are not meant to be gobbled by the handful, so watch portion control.

FRUIT YOGURT Yogurts that feature fruit at the bottom also contain extra sugar and preservatives. Stick with plain or vanilla varieties for your probiotic protein boost, and try adding fresh fruit, nuts, or flaxseeds.

PITA CHIPS Watch out, consumers—these so-called healthy snack chips can have as much fat and sodium as a bag of name-brand corn chips. Look for baked and seasoned varieties rather than fried, salty ones.

LO-CAL FROZEN MEALS Most of us love the convenience of popping a low-calorie dinner into a microwave. But not only do many frozen meals contain high levels of sodium, they also short-change diners on greens, with their small portions of limp, waterlogged veggies. Consider augmenting your meal with a salad or a serving of vegetables or fruit.

PACKAGED SANDWICH MEAT Some of these sliced meats have fewer calories than their deli-counter counterparts because they are packed with water, but they can also be very salty, especially those with smoky or peppery flavorings. Plain turkey or chicken are your best options.

FRUIT JUICE When it comes to increasing your intake of vegetables and fruits, as recommended, drinking fruit juice is one convenient solution. Unfortunately, many juices contain only marginal amounts of real fruit juice, if any, and most 100 percent fruit juices have had the beneficial fiber removed.

LO-CAL SALAD DRESSING Any foods with low-fat or fat-free labels are holdovers from days when saturated fat was falsely vilified. Manufacturers found that removing fat also removed flavor, which they made up by adding copious amounts of sugar. Simply use smaller portions of dressing or sour cream, rather than "diet" varieties.

CANNED SOUP This is "old news" in the nutrition world— canned soup may be good, but it is also loaded with salt. Try buying low-sodium soup and seasoning it with a little salt and the savory flavors of black or red pepper and spices, like basil, oregano, cilantro, cumin, or dill.

BROWN RICE Whole-grain brown rice offers more health benefits than white rice and is more filling, but it's not high on taste. Try combining whole grains with rice or regular pasta, and season the mix with herbs and spices.

PLAN AHEAD

One way to help ensure the effectiveness of a fitness program is to prepare a weekly diet plan. Take your pick of diet plan templates on the internet; many offer food and portion suggestions along with easy-to-prepare recipes. Once you have selected a plan, create a shopping list. If some recipes can be made ahead and frozen, get them ready before you start the plan. In addition to breakfast, lunch, and dinner, be sure the plan includes a few between-meal snacks for "grazing." Many nutritionists concur that consuming multiple small meals a day is healthier than the traditional three large meals. If the plan is still not satisfying you after two weeks, or you aren't getting the results you hoped for, try another plan, perhaps one with more emphasis on vegetables or juicing. And, of course, before embarking on any serious weight-loss regimen, always consult with a doctor first.

SIT DOWN!

We all do it—standing over the sink as we spoon up our oatmeal or grabbing a health bar for lunch as we rush to a meeting or gazing into the open refrigerator as we spoon down the ice cream. But, dining on our feet or on the run is not conducive to proper digestion. It is also makes it too easy to indulge in poor dietary habits. Mealtimes need to be acknowledged with a proper setting along with the proper amount of time allotted for you to slowly consume—and chew—your food.

So set the table, dim the lights, and put on relaxing music—even if it's only a date with yourself! And if you must eat on the run, invest in a bullet blender, and make healthy fruit and veggie smoothies to sip as you drive.

SHAVE PORTIONS

Reducing your calorie intake by about 20 percent is part of a good initial fitness routine. Here are a number of tricks that can help you eat less and resist going back for seconds.

FILL UP Drink a 16-ounce (480 ml) glass of water before mealtime. A full belly makes you less likely to overindulge.

ADJUST RATIOS Add nutrient-rich veggies and fruits to your recipes to make up for reduced portions of protein, fat, and carbs. Add spinach to pasta, extra green beans to stir fries, apple slices to cereal, or switch mushrooms for half the meat in ground-meat recipes.

CONTROL PORTIONS Never snack on foods right out of the bag or box—it's impossible to control intake, and studies say you can eat 50 percent more than you intended. If a snack package contains six servings, then divide it up into six zip bags.

FOOL THE EYE Use a smaller dinner plate than normal to fool your eyes into thinking your portion size has not shrunk. Put mixed drinks or cocktails in tall, thin glasses with extra ice to make them appear more substantial—and limit yourself to one.

CIRCLE THE BUFFET Look over the buffet offerings before deciding on what to choose to put on your plate. In studies, diners often put the first three things they saw on their plates, regardless of calories.

CONTRAST COLORS You are more likely to take bigger servings when the food color is similar to the color of the plate—white Alfredo pasta on white plates, for instance. So if you serve red meat, opt for pale plates, and with chicken or fish, use your darkest stoneware.

START WITH SOUP Research shows that when diners begin a meal with a brothlike soup, such as a consommé, they tend to consume less food overall.

SATISFY CRAVINGS Satisfy your craving for dessert at the end of a meal with a flavorful decaf tea like peppermint, chocolate, or raspberry peach.

STAY BUTTONED UP Fitted, more rigid clothing such as blue jeans, dress pants, or a tailored jacket will feel increasingly tighter as you continue to eat and warn you when to put down the fork. Don't just unbutton for comfort—stop eating!

PAY ATTENTION Concentrate on your meals. Don't watch TV or play computer games while you eat—you are likely to end up consuming more food while feeling less satisfied.

THINK *about it*
Differentiate between cravings and hunger. If you can comprehend the difference between wanting to eat and actually needing to eat, you can more easily eliminate unnecessary calories.

CARRY YOUR OWN SNACKS

The healthiest option when you're traveling is to bring your own snacks. Try these tasty treats, which are inexpensive and easy to tote along wherever you go.

PACK DRIED SNACKS Prepare individual servings of dried fruit; be sure to follow the serving size on the package label.

KEEP YOUR COOL For car travel, bring a small cooler with fresh fruit, such as apples, oranges, bananas, or grapes.

BRING THE GREENS Cut up raw veggies and carry them in a snap-lid bowl; they provide fiber and a nice crunch.

CHILL OUT Freeze individual cartons of low-fat yogurt ahead of time for a refreshing, gut-healthy treat.

BAG YOUR BREAKFAST Pour single servings of your favorite high-fiber cereal into sealable sandwich bags.

TAKE A CUP WITH YOU Invest in an insulated travel mug so you can indulge in homemade smoothies while you are on the go.

PACK A LUNCH Assemble a complete, healthy meal, including snacks, in storage containers, and store them in an insulated lunch box or cooler that you can toss in your back seat. Just be sure to pull over when you want to enjoy it!

THINK about it
Don't forget to hit the gym if your travel plans allow it. You can find Gold's Gyms throughout the U.S. and in many countries internationally. And many hotels have their own gyms or fitness centers.

ORDER WISELY

When dining out, it isn't always easy to make smart, healthful choices, especially when you're looking over a multi-page menu full of tempting items. The following guidelines could help you to stay on-plan.

GET IN THE CLEAR Begin with a clear, vegetable-based soup or side salad to reduce your appetite.

ASK FOR IT ON THE SIDE Always ask for salad dressing on the side, so that you can control how much you use.

LIMIT THE BREAD If the bread basket calls your name, eat one small piece with a drizzle of olive oil instead of butter.

LOSE THE FAT Avoid anything called crispy: that means "fried."

CHOOSE THE COOKING METHOD Opt for meats that are grilled, baked, broiled, roasted, or braised.

OPT FOR LEAN Order lean cuts of beef, like T-bone, sirloin, flank or strip steak, and pot roast. Or choose poultry or seafood.

DON'T GIVE IN TO TRENDS Don't cave in to "fad" foods of processed or fatty meat, like pork belly or short ribs; they are not worth the caloric beating you will take.

ORDER À LA CARTE Consider ordering salad and soup à la carte and then sharing a main course with a companion.

KNOW THE FACTS If you're dining at a chain restaurant, look up the menu online beforehand to get the nutritional info you need to make informed choices.

EAT LIKE A KID Remember that in many places, adults can order off the kid's menu. Sometimes that's just enough comfort food to satisfy you without trouncing your diet.

Ask the EXPERT

DO I HAVE TO SKIP DESSERT?

There's not much good to say about sugary foods—when following a fitness plan, avoid or limit processed foods and sugar. These empty calories offer nothing in the way of nutrition.

We all know that sticking to a fitness and nutrition regimen isn't easy. If you've been vigilant and eating clean, a little reward for all that hard work will probably do you more good than harm. You can go ahead and order that dessert, but be sure you partake in this kind of indulgence no more than once a week. You can even schedule in a regular cheat meal—just anticipating your weekly splurge can help ease the stress of sticking with the program.

EAT SMART ON THE GO

So you've been exercising hard and watching your diet—and results are beginning to show. But once holiday or summer travel season shows up, you may find your good habits are at risk. Here are some safe bets for eating healthy on the go and what to steer clear of in a few common travel situations.

HOW TO ...	SAFE BET	STEER CLEAR
SNACK SMART WHILE YOU WAIT	When your only choice for a snack is a terminal or train station newsstand, opt for trail mix or a low-fat, high-protein energy bar. But follow the serving size on trail mix—it's typically about a cup (57 g) or a palmful—and pass on what's left to a neighbor to avoid calorie overload.	If an upscale coffee shop is an option, beware of added calorie traps that come with drinks. Whole milk, flavored syrups, and whipped cream can add 300 or more calories to your beverage. Instead choose bottled water to stay hydrated while traveling.
CONTROL CALORIES ON A FLIGHT	Some airlines offer economy passengers a snack box that contains tuna, hummus, baked pita chips, raisins, and organic crackers—all adding up to around 600 calories. Consider sharing it—and the calories—with a travel companion. Other airlines offer a turkey sandwich with light mayo that comes with a bag of baby carrots and a small candy bar. Or you might order an energy bar that's high in protein, but only contains 200 calories. Check your airline's website to see what sort of healthful options they have for fitness-conscious travelers.	Avoid salty snacks, which dehydrate you in the already dry cabin air. Also beware of high-sugar, high-fat treats that pack the equivalent calories of a meal but leave you feeling unsatisfied.
EAT RIGHT ON THE ROAD	For a quick bite, stop at a mini mart, and head to the refrigerator section for low-fat string cheese, fat-free yogurt, or fresh fruit. For a meal, look for fast food restaurants that offer salads with grilled—not fried—chicken and low-fat or fat-free dressing. A baked potato topped with chili is a good way to get 15 percent of your daily serving of fiber. Pair it with water and lemon or unsweetened iced tea. Compared to a 20-ounce (290 ml) regular soda, this option will save more than 200 calories.	Avoid anything that's extra meaty, extra-crispy, slathered in gravy or melted cheese, super-sized, fried, or sugary.
TAILOR YOUR RESTAURANT MEALS	When dining in unfamiliar surroundings, check the menu for baked or broiled chicken or fish and steamed veggies. Don't be afraid to ask questions: "How is that prepared?" "What's the vegetable of the day?" or "Can I get a baked potato instead of fries?"	Avoid consuming oversized portions: split a large entrée with your travel companion—otherwise, high-fat, high-calorie items will leave you feeling guilty, sluggish, and sleepy for the rest of your trip.
KEEP IT HEALTHY AT THE BEACH	You are on vacation to relax, unwind, and enjoy, not to stress out or feel guilty after making bad food choices. Start the day off with a filling breakfast—an egg-white omelet with fruit and whole-wheat toast—to avoid making a bad decision at the beachside café. Stay hydrated with water and fresh-fruit smoothies.	Be careful of poolside snacks—you'll want to save those excess calories for a satisfying dinner.

STAY HYDRATED

Water is critical to human life, flushing our tissues and aiding metabolism. Some sports medicine specialists believe that half the population is mildly dehydrated at any given time. Sadly, these people don't even know they are dehydrated, having so rarely felt the benefits of true hydration. During workouts, when your body loses fluids through sweat, it's even more important to take frequent breaks with the water bottle.

Dehydration, especially if caused by intense physical activity like exercise, can decrease strength, endurance, and performance or skill levels in sports. Every cell and organ system in your body has to work harder, and because there is less blood volume, the cardiovascular system raises your heart rate to compensate. A properly hydrated individual, on the other hand, displays better decision-making skills, higher levels of concentration, elevated mood, and increased coordination. The following guidelines will help keep you hydrated during your normal busy days, as well as on your workout days.

EVERY DAY Drink eight 8-ounce (240 ml) glasses of water every day.

BEFORE AND AFTER WORKOUTS Drink 12 to 24 ounces (355–710 ml) of water before and after a workout.

DURING WORKOUTS Drink 8 ounces (240 ml) of water every 20 minutes during a workout.

DURING EXTENDED WORKOUTS For extended workouts lasting more than an hour, combine water with low-calorie sports drinks that replace lost electrolytes and provide sugar for energy.

CURB THE CAFFEINE

Drinking coffee or black tea does not count as part of your daily water requirement—the caffeine in these beverages acts as a diuretic, flushing water from your body. The famous "caffeine rush" may give you a false sense of energy when you are feeling tired or fatigued, but caffeine is a stimulant that will ultimately leave you feeling even more run-down after it peaks.

A small amount can ease headaches, but too much can actually trigger them. If you want to limit caffeine, cut back gradually until you indulge only two days a week. If you must use caffeine to boost your metabolism—studies show that coffee and green tea do have this effect—be aware that coffee has a half-life of 6.5 hours. If you plan to turn in by 10:00 p.m., stop drinking coffee by 2:30 p.m., so that you have at least an hour with no caffeine in your system.

TRY TEA

Want a hot beverage that won't produce all the side effects of caffeinated drinks? Try herbal teas. These can come in a multitude of tasty varieties, including blackberry, ginger, rose hip, hibiscus flower, peppermint, chamomile, lemon balm, and more. There are herbal teas to wake you up, those to calm you before bedtime, and even those to serve as dessert. Many herbal teas contain vitamin C and antioxidants, and some can aid digestion and respiration.

When served plain, herbal teas add zero calories to your diet. That makes them excellent "craving quenchers" to sip while you watch TV, work on the computer, or cook dinner. And don't forget to try them iced for summertime refreshment before, during, or after a workout.

Commercial herbal teas can be purchased in most supermarkets, or check out a health food shop for more unusual or healthful varieties.

GO GREEN

When you crave a caffeinated beverage, it's definitely smart to go green … as in green tea, one of the healthiest drinks around. Its chock-full of antioxidants and nutrients that have powerfully beneficial effects on your body.

Among the many claims made for this tea: it can improve brain function, promote fat loss, and boost the metabolism. Just remember, however, that like other caffeinated beverages, green tea can act as a diuretic.

Whatever the claims, green tea is delicious either hot or cold. Just be sure to buy quality organic green tea or order it at restaurants that brew it fresh. Beware of canned and bottled varieties with added flavors—often those flavors also add sugars and calories.

GLOSSARY

aerobic Relating to activity that increases the body's demand for oxygen thereby resulting in temporary increase in breathing and heart rate.

ambience A feeling or mood associated with a particular place.

amenities Something that helps provide comfort, convenience, or enjoyment.

bodybuilder A person who develops their physique through diet and exercise for competitions.

certified Officially recognized as holding certain qualifications.

compression The act of pressing or squeezing together.

discipline Control gained by enforcing obedience or order.

endurance The ability to sustain a prolonged stressful effort or activity.

enzyme Any of numerous complex proteins that are produced by living cells and catalyze specific biochemical reactions at body temperatures.

indicator Something that provides evidence on the state or condition of something.

multitasking Performing several jobs at once.

physique The form, size, and development of a person's body.

priority Something given or meriting attention before competing alternatives.

regimen A systematic plan to improve and maintain health.

resistance The power or capacity to resist, or push away.

sedentary Not physically active.

stimulate To raise levels of activity in something.

strenuous Vigorously active.

versatility The quality of having many uses or applications.

wicking Able to keep out fluid or moisture.

FURTHER READING

BOOKS

Anatomy of Fitness Personal Training and Workout Diary.
   Heatherton, Australia: Hinkler Books Ltd, 2012.

Powers, Scott K., and Stephen L. Dodd. *Total Fitness and
   Wellness, the Mastering Health Edition.* London, UK:
   Pearson. 2016.

Sharkey, Brian J., and Steven E. Gaskill. *Fitness & Health.*
   Champaign, IL: Human Kinetics Publishers, 2013.

WEBSITES
Monitor Your Progress
https://www.girlshealth.gov/fitness/started/plan.html
Discover how to create and maintain a healthy fitness plan.

Physical Activity and Health
*https://www.hhs.gov/fitness/be-active/importance-of-
physical-activity/index.html*
Learn about the risks of a sedentary lifestyle and why
fitness is so important.

Steps to Get Started
*https://www.mayoclinic.org/healthy-lifestyle/fitness/
in-depth/fitness/art-20048269*
Read about assessing your current fitness level to create a
new plan.

INDEX

V

vegan protein sources, 29
vitamin D, 32, 33

W

warming up, 24
water bottle, 22
weight-lifting gloves, 22
workout journal, 23
workout profile, 14–15

Y

yoga, 7, 8, 12, 15